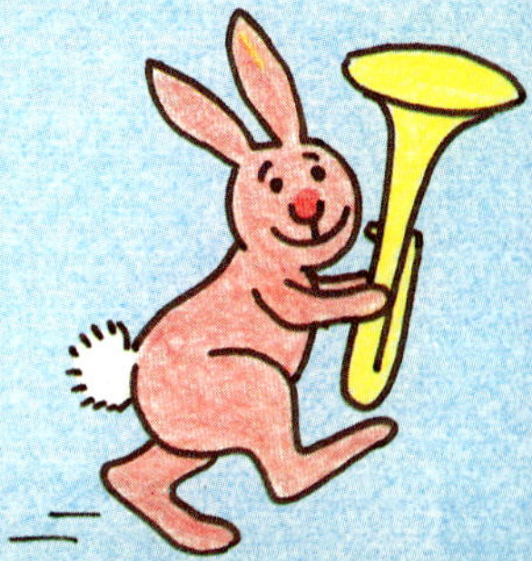

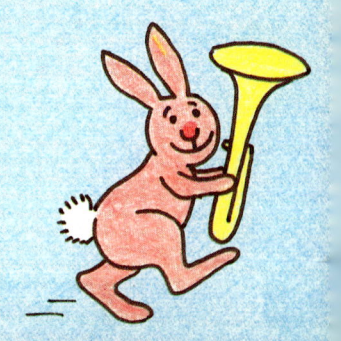

How Do I Breathe?

by Ulrik Hvass

Illustrated by Volker Theinhardt

VIKING KESTREL

What happens when you breathe? You take in air, blow it out, and then take in air again.

When your dog has been running, he pants. He breathes loudly and quickly and his tongue hangs out. Running might make you a bit out of breath too!

Where does the air you breathe go to? Put your hand flat on your chest. When you breathe deeply, you can feel your chest moving in and out.

Put your ear against a friend's back and ask her to take deep breaths.
You can hear the sound of air moving as she breathes in and out.

Inside your body the air goes into two spongy bags which are called your lungs. They can blow up and deflate just like balloons.

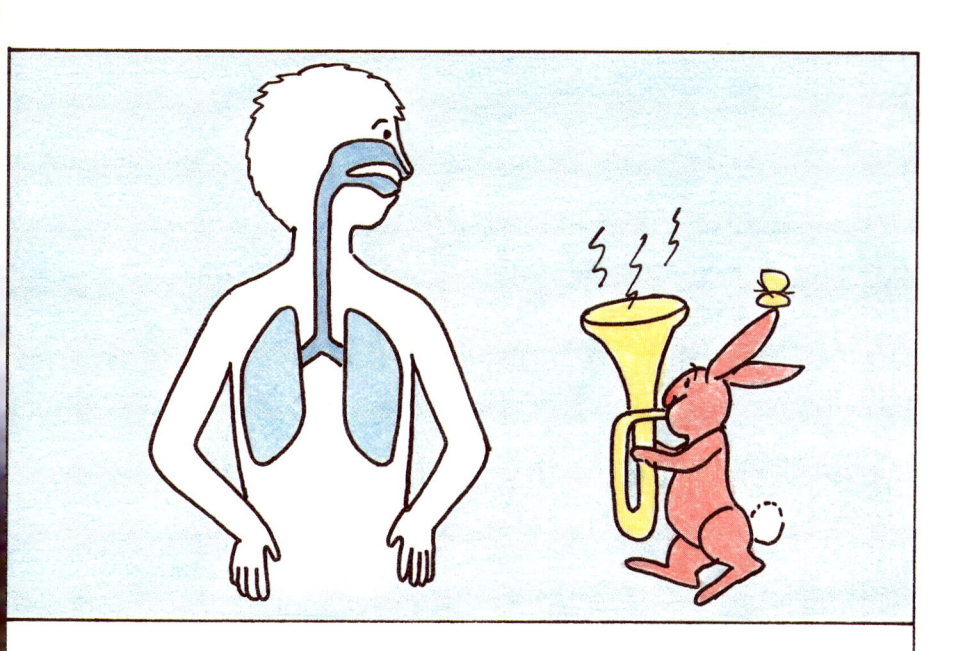

One lung is on the right side and the other is on the left side of your chest. A tube, called the windpipe, carries the air you breathe into your body. It then divides into two branches, one for the left lung and one for the right.

Why do we breathe?

If you put your face underwater when you are in the bath, you soon have to take it out to breathe. Otherwise you'd drown. You have to breathe air to stay alive.

Is the air that you blow out of your lungs the same as the air you breathed in?

No, something has happened to the air and it's different, even though you can't see it because air is invisible.

Blow onto a cold window. What happens? Small drops of water form on the glass. This shows that the air you breathe out contains water vapor or steam.

Here's an experiment to show you another difference between the air you breathe in and out. You'll need two identical glass jars, two candles, and some matches.

Ask a grown-up to help you light the candles. Jar number 1 is full of the air from the room. Take jar number 2 and, with your mouth close to the opening, breathe deeply into it several times. You'll thus fill up the jar with the air that comes out of your lungs.

Now at the same time quickly cover one candle with jar number 1 and the other with jar number 2. What happens? The candle under jar number 2 goes out first. Something is missing in the air you breathe out that would have made the candle burn longer. How has the air changed? The air has changed even though you can't see any difference.

Take one of the jars again and let it fill up with the air from the room. Put the jar over one of the candles. As soon as the candle goes out, put the same jar quickly over the other candle. The second candle will go out almost at once.

In order to burn, candles need something from the air. It's called oxygen. The second candle went out quickly because the first candle had used up all the oxygen in the air. In the other experiment your lungs had already taken the oxygen from the jar when you breathed in and out of it and that's why that second candle went out.

What happens to the oxygen that goes to your lungs? If it just stayed there, then breathing in would make you swell up like a balloon.

The oxygen does stay inside your body, but it doesn't stay in your lungs. Instead, the oxygen goes into the blood.

When you've been running fast, put your hand on your heart. You'll feel it beating faster for a while. When you run, it's not only your legs that you use, but your heart beats faster and your lungs breathe faster too. You need more oxygen when your body is working hard.

In a laboratory you can test to see what happens when oxygen is made to bubble into dark red blood. The blood becomes bright red. It's the oxygen in your blood which makes it a bright red color. Blood becomes dark red again when there's not much oxygen left in it.

If you blow air through a straw into limewater (a clear solution of calcium hydroxide in water), the limewater turns white. This shows that there is another kind of gas in the air you breathe out. Its name is carbon dioxide. There was almost no carbon dioxide in the air you breathed in before it entered your lungs.

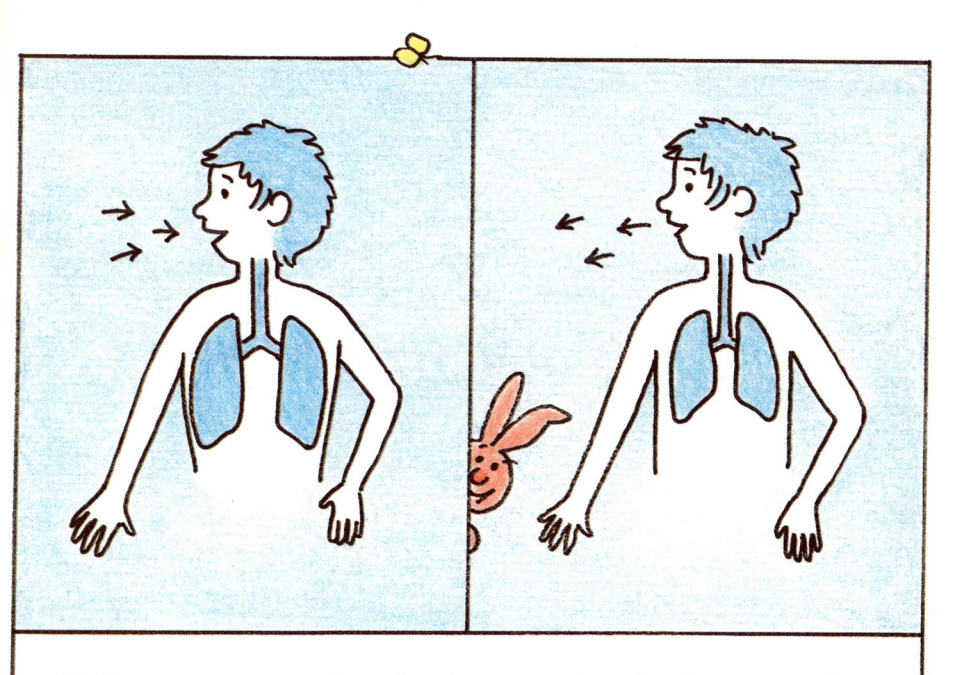

All these experiments show that the air you breathe changes inside your lungs.

You keep the oxygen and it goes into your blood. You breathe out water vapor and carbon dioxide.

You breathe all the time even if you don't notice that you're doing it. You need the oxygen that's in the air in order to live.

VIKING KESTREL
Viking Penguin Inc., 40 West 23rd Street, New York, New York 10010, U.S.A.
Penguin Books Ltd, Harmondsworth, Middlesex, England
Penguin Books Australia Ltd, Ringwood, Victoria, Australia
Penguin Books Canada Limited, 2801 John Street, Markham, Ontario, Canada L3R 1B4
Penguin Books (N.Z.) Ltd, 182-190 Wairau Road, Auckland 10, New Zealand

Translation copyright © Éditions du Centurion, Paris, 1986
All rights reserved

First published in France as *La Respiration* by
Éditions du Centurion, 1986. © 1986, Éditions du Centurion, Paris.
This English-language edition first published in 1986 by Viking Penguin Inc.
Published simultaneously in Canada
Printed in France by Offset Aubin, Poitiers
1 2 3 4 5 90 89 88 87 86

Library of Congress catalog card number: 86-40004
(CIP data available)
ISBN 0-670-81196-3

Without limiting the rights under copyright reserved above, no part of this
publication may be reproduced, stored in or introduced into a retrieval system,
or transmitted, in any form or by any means (electronic, mechanical, photocopying,
recording or otherwise), without the prior written permission of both the
copyright owner and the above publisher of this book.

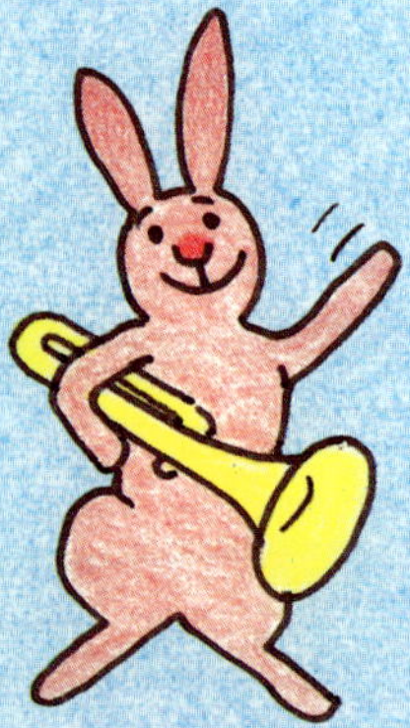